Disclaimer Notice:
Please note the information contained within this document is for educational and entertainment purposes only. Every attempt has been made to provide accurate, up to date and reliable complete information. No warranties of any kind are expressed or implied.
Please consult a licensed professional before attempting any techniques outlined in this book. By reading this document, the reader agrees that under no circumstances is the author responsible for any losses, direct or indirect, which are incurred as a result of the use of information contained within this document, including, but not limited to, errors, omissions, or inaccuracies.

ISBN 978-0-473-67983-5 Paperback
ISBN 978-0-473-67984-2 Kindle
ISBN 978-0-473-67985-9 Audiobook

CONTENTS

For Hayley, Hope and Max

Preface

The experience of psychological trauma can have debilitating effects on those who have stumbled across its path. For friends, family, colleagues, and professionals who live and work alongside people who have been hurt by trauma, it is distressing to feel helpless or unsure about what to do for the best.

This easy-to-read book 'Introduction to Trauma' is a way of bringing together my work as a Clinical Psychologist and University Teacher. My intention is that this will be a valuable resource for you. In the first chapter I will introduce you to the team. Each of the characters in the Trauma Team has a special gift to share and will help you to remember the key things to bear in mind when supporting someone who is healing from trauma.

PART ONE
INTRODUCTIONS

Hello from Professor Brainy

Hello. I am Professor Brainy. I have spent a lot of time studying people's brains.

I am interested in what happens to people's brains when they experience things that are very stressful and frightening.

When something dangerous happens and you feel like you or someone close to you might die or be very badly hurt, this is known as a trauma.

Because it is such a horrible thing to happen, afterwards lots of people don't feel safe, and can get angry or sad and find it difficult to get to sleep because they have nightmares.

Other people they live and work with might not understand the changes they see in their friend, or family member.

Teachers at school and colleagues at work might misunderstand the person's behaviour and think they don't care, or they are being deliberately naughty, or that they should be punished.

Professor Brainy is good at explaining complicated things about what happens when people experience terrible things.

She also has six special helpers in her Trauma Team. Three helpers are in the Understanding Gang and three helpers are in the Change Family.

Throughout this book the people in the Understanding Gang and the Change Family will talk to you about each of the six gifts that they have to share

Professor Brainy and her team have written this book together so that we can all work together to support people who have experienced trauma to get better.

The Understanding Gang

The Understanding Gang help us to understand what someone who has experienced trauma needs. There are three gifts that the Understanding Gang offer: Choice, Predictability and Safety.

These gifts show you how to create an environment for the person you are supporting that will help them feel safe and understood.

The Understanding Gang understand what it is like to go through things that are traumatic.

They explain things to help us have more compassion and empathy with people who have experienced trauma.

The Understanding Gang show us how to let the person we are supporting know that the difficulties or problems they may be struggling with now, make sense because of what has happened to them in the past. They each bring a different gift of understanding.

The Understanding Gang have learned about trauma-responsive care[i]. Trauma responsive means to understand that people's behaviour that we don't like is not always because the person wants to act like that.

If someone has experienced trauma, their behaviour is usually not because there is something wrong ***with*** them. It is usually because they are struggling to heal from something bad that has happened ***to*** them.

Instead of asking what is wrong with someone, the Trauma Team teach us to ask

"What happened to you?"

Hello from Charlie Choosey

Hello I am Charlie Choosey.

The gift I bring is to explain the importance of giving people who have experienced trauma choices.

One of the most horrible things about traumatic situations is to have no control or choice about what is happening.

When something very frightening happens, the person has little or no choice about what they can do to help themselves to escape.

Charlie Choosey shows us ways to allow the person we are supporting to make their own choices, when they are with us, when they are on their own, and when they are with other people.

Hello from Penny Predictable

Hello I am Penny Predictable.

The gift I bring is to show you how to be more predictable.

People who have experienced trauma may be frightened of change and surprises.

They often prefer to know what is going to happen in advance.

Instead of changing our plans at the last minute or not telling someone what to expect, Penny Predictable gives us tips and ideas about making what we do predictable and consistent.

Hello from Sam Safety

Hello I am Sam Safety.

The gift I bring is to remind you to think about the different ways we can help someone to feel safe.

When a person experienced something traumatic, they felt very unsafe at the time, and even after it is over, they still feel unsafe.

Sam Safety teaches us about the gift of safety.

He explains that we can do this by showing someone the different ways we have thought about helping them feel safe. Safe when they are with us, when they are on their own or with other people.

The Change Family

The Change Family teach us how to make helpful lifestyle changes to support the healing of someone who has experienced trauma. There are three gifts that the Change Family offer: Bravery, Calm, and Noticing.

Their gifts are ways of helping a person who has experienced trauma to heal and grow. It is important to keep in balance the gifts from the Understanding Gang and those from the Change Family.

The Change Family offer lots of love and support. They are willing to share their gifts to help people heal and grow after trauma.

When people have experienced trauma, some of the things they experience are dissociation, avoidance, and hyperarousal.

The Change Family each bring their special gifts to support someone who is experiencing these symptoms.

They don't want to see the person they care about suffering or be in pain, and they offer their advice and suggestions in a loving way.

After following the advice of the Understanding Gang, the guidance from the Change Family can be shared.

This way, the person who has experience trauma can make the difficult changes in their life that will give them hope and freedom. They can start to make changes when they feel understood.

Hello from Baby Brave

Hello, I am Baby Brave.

The gift I bring is that I never avoid people or things because I am scared of them.

I can help you to be braver with the gift of facing up to things that are scary. I give the gift of courage and trust and confidence that even difficult things can get better.

Baby Brave wants to learn and grow and always wants to ask questions and investigate things.

Baby Brave is so curious about what is going on, and crawls around all over the place bravely examining and exploring new things and old things.

Hello from Cousin Calm

Hello, I am Cousin Calm.

The gift that I bring is that I am very good at helping people feel calm and relaxed.

I can sing and cook and like to meditate and play football.

I hope to offer you some advice about how to switch off from worrying about things and get a good night's sleep.

Cousin Calm is great to have around because just being with him makes people feel better.

He also gives the gift of companionship and makes sure no one feels lonely or left out.

Hello from Nana Noticing

Hello I am Nana Noticing.

The gift I bring is that I notice everything! I notice smells, sounds, tastes and texture of things.

I also notice how I am feeling and what I am thinking. I notice what other people are doing and how I react to other people and situations.

When she shares her gift, Nana Noticing helps people to stay in the here-and-now and not to disconnect from what is going on around them and float off into a daydream.

Balancing Understanding and Change

Now that we have met everyone in the Understanding Gang and the Change Family, let's think about how they work together.

Sometimes it is called balancing acceptance and change, or balancing validation and change. We need both.

It is helpful to imagine them all sitting on a seesaw so that you remember that you need everyone to keep the balance.

PART TWO
THE UNDERSTANDING GANG

Each person in the Understanding Gang has a gift of understanding, and they will take it in turns in to share that with you.

One way of thinking about what makes the Understanding Gang so understanding is that they have learned about something called trauma-informed care. Sometimes this is also called trauma-responsive care.

Understanding glasses

Being trauma-informed is like wearing 'understanding' glasses to watch what someone is doing.

Without these glasses someone's behaviour may not make sense, and we might call them 'naughty', or 'bad', or 'disrespectful' or 'unsociable'. When we think of someone's behaviour in this way, we tend to treat people unkindly.

We might think the best way to make them act better is to punish them for behaviour we don't like, and reward them for behaviour we do like.

However, this can often just make the person feel more misunderstood and can actually cause them to experience more pain and suffering. When someone is in pain they often say and do things that they would not normally do when they are feeling okay.

The Understanding Gang have learned about the effects that psychological trauma can have on someone. Because of this, they have some gifts to share with you about how to put on the trauma-informed understanding glasses.

Experiencing psychological trauma causes a lot of damage to a person, just like experiencing a physical trauma such as a broken leg or a deep cut. The difference is that psychological trauma is inside the body and the brain, and we can't see it.

It is easier to be understanding and compassionate to someone who we can see has a broken leg and is struggling to walk or do ordinary things in life.

We understand if they are grumpy or irritable, that it is because they are hurting.

The same is true of someone who is hurting on the inside. The problem is that when the injury is inside someone, we can't see it. So, it might be more difficult to be understanding and compassionate when they are struggling to do ordinary things in life, or if they are grumpy and impatient.

When you understand why someone is behaving the way they are, it is much easier to help them and to give them the right kind of support that will allow them to heal and grow.

The gift from the Understanding Gang to you is to give you some 'understanding glasses' so you can see why someone who has experienced trauma might be acting as they are.

They also share some helpful practical suggestions about what you can do to support someone who has experienced trauma so that they can heal and grow.

UNDERSTANDING TRAUMA
WITH
PENNY PREDICTABLE

Penny Predictable understands that someone who has experienced trauma needs other people to be consistent and predictable

The gift Penny Predictable brings is to show us how it can help someone who has experienced trauma when we are predictable and consistent.

Everyone is different. Penny Predictable understands that people who have experienced traumatic, frightening and very distressing things in their lives can feel more vulnerable than people who haven't.

Adverse Childhood Events

Lots of research has been done to find out what life experiences can make someone more vulnerable. These often happen early in life and are called Adverse Childhood Events - abbreviated to ACEs. These are different kinds of trauma.

Examples are parental separation, being looked after in Care, childhood abuse, neglect, a parent in prison, or growing up with parents or a family member with problematic drug or alcohol use.

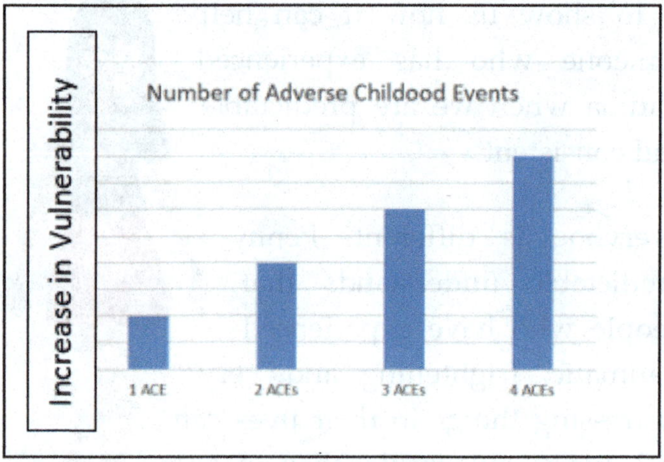

The more adverse events children experience, the more vulnerable they are. You can see in this graph that someone's 'vulnerability' increases every time they experience another Adverse Event.

Vulnerability is the opposite of resilience.

Vulnerability

Penny Predictable explains that one way of thinking about vulnerability is to imagine different sizes of buckets. The buckets represent resilience, or the ability to cope well with difficult things.

The more ACEs someone experiences, the smaller and smaller their bucket gets.

No ACEs One Two Three Four ACEs

That means, it becomes more and more difficult to cope well with difficult things in life.

Imagine that new difficult, stressful, or challenging things people encounter in life are like pouring water into the bucket.

Every difficult situation is like a big splosh of water in the bucket.

People who are very resilient have large strong buckets, but people who are more vulnerable may only have tiny buckets. That means the vulnerable people get overwhelmed with difficult circumstances more quickly than the resilient people.

The same difficulty or same sized splosh of water is much harder for someone with a small bucket to manage than someone with a larger bucket.

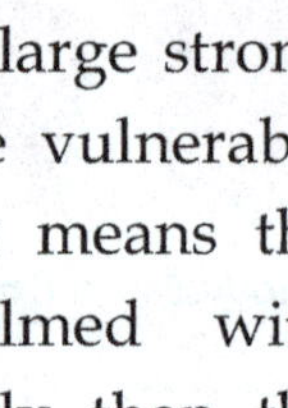

This is also called the 'stress-vulnerability' model[ii]. It's not their fault, it's just that life circumstances have shrunk their bucket!

Other things that might make someone vulnerable and have a smaller coping bucket are poor health, low income, and discrimination.

People who have smaller coping buckets are less resilient to stress and are more vulnerable to being overwhelmed.

Resilience

The opposite of vulnerability is something called 'resilience'. Most people are quite resilient to traumatic experiences[iii].

The dictionary defines resilience as the ability to "*recover quickly from difficulties*" or "*spring back into shape*"[iv] .

Penny Predictable explains that this means a person can 'bounce back' and return to doing the things they were doing before the trauma relatively quickly[v].

There are three things that make a difference to how resilient a person is. The three things that influence how resilient someone is are shown in the following triangle diagram.

Triangle of resilience

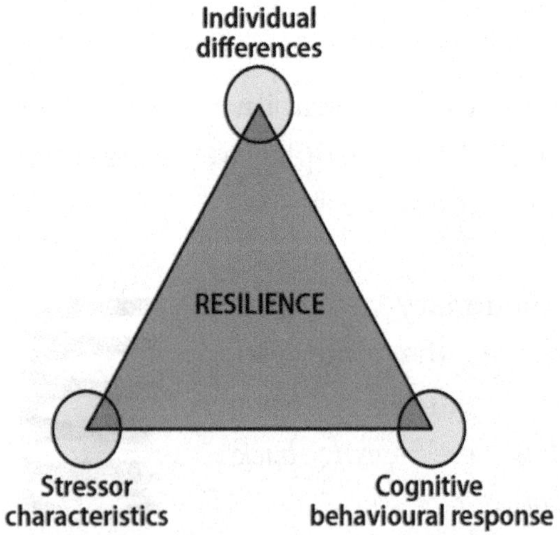

Each of these three things is explained in more detail in the table on the next page.

Explanation of the three things that affect how resilient someone is.

Individual differences	Personal differences such as personality, health, and how past experiences such as ACEs have affected their view of the world.
Stressor characteristics	Things about the situation or event that are stressful, frightening or distressing. Some situations are more difficult than others
Cognitive behavioural responses	How a person typically responds to stressful situations. This means the automatic thoughts and actions someone has learned.

Penny Predictable knows is that a way to help people with small coping buckets is to make some holes in the bottom of the bucket.

This means that when the big sploshes of water from difficult things in life come along, some of it can drain away instead of overflowing.

In other words, Penny Predictable explains that we can teach people who have experienced trauma extra ways to manage difficult things.

This helps them not to get overwhelmed a life is a bit easier for them.

The holes in the bucket mean that even if lots of stressful things pour into the bucket, some of it can drain away.

There are things a person can do to help poke some holes in their bucket to let the stress out.

These might be resting, exercising, getting fresh air, eating more fruit and vegetables, spending time with people you like to be with or doing fun things.

For people with bigger buckets, they can cope much better with change, uncertainty, and inconsistency.

However, the gift that Penny Predictable gives is an understanding that people who have experienced trauma have a smaller ability to cope with uncertainty and change.

Penny Predictable says

A person who is vulnerable because of trauma, can be thought of as having a small coping bucket.

Penny Predictable says that a great way to make a hole for someone else in their small coping bucket is to be predictable, reliable, and consistent.

That means the person is less stressed because they know what to expect from you.

Tips from Penny Predictable

- If you make an appointment, keep it and don't cancel it or move it.
- Keep your meetings or lessons as regular as possible
- Make a calendar with times you will meet marked on it.
- Before you do anything explain what you are planning, and check it is okay.
- Have a structure. For example, start with a drink and end with relaxation.
- Avoid doing unexpected things.
- If you say you will do something, make sure you do. If you say you won't, don't.

UNDERSTANDING TRAUMA WITH SAM SAFETY

Sam Safety understands that someone who has experienced trauma needs to feel safe

The gift Sam Safety brings is to reminds us about the different ways we can help someone else to feel safe.

Experts say the main problem with experiencing trauma is feeling unsafe[vi].

That is why helping someone feel safe is always an important starting point in supporting someone who has experienced trauma.

If someone has experienced a lot of horrible, dangerous, and stressful things in their life, they can start to think that it is impossible to be safe.

Sam Safety has some great ideas about how to help someone feel safe on their own, with other people and when they meet you.

Sally Scared

This is Sally Scared.

When she doesn't feel safe, she feels very scared and stressed.

When people feel scared or stressed it is difficult for them to concentrate on what you are saying.

It is hard for people to remember things when they feel scared. It is also hard for them to learn anything.

It is a wise thing to help someone feel safe before you start trying to explain anything or ask them to do something.

Sam Safety says

Some people have lots of hurtful things happen to them when they are young, and may not remember ever having a time when they felt safe and okay.

Other people may have had a life where most of the time they were safe and cared for. So, when a traumatic thing happens to them, it is a huge shock that changes the way they think about themselves, other people, and the world.

Imagine having an idea about the world being safe, because that is all you have ever experienced. Then an accident happens, or someone harms you.

The person who has experienced this now has two different things to try to make sense of. One is "I thought the world was a safe place", and the other is "My new experience teaches me the world is not a safe place".

The old way of thinking doesn't match with the new experience. Because of this, people usually change the way they think. In other words, they change what they believe about themselves, other people and the world.

A theory in psychology that explains the process of changing beliefs is called 'shattered assumptions[vii].' This means the expectations, and thoughts about the world and other people the person used to believe are now broken, or shattered.

Helping someone feel safe is a place to start working out how to pick up all the broken pieces and put them together in a new way.

It won't be the same as before, but feeling safe helps someone to think logically.

Creating safety builds trust

When a person has been hurt by other people, they start to lose trust, because when they trusted someone in the past, they got hurt.

This is one of the reasons that they stopped feeling safe.

Helping someone feel safe is also a way of helping them be able to trust themselves and other people who care about them.

Sam Safety's first gift is an easy way to remember the five types of safety. People need to feel safe in their relationships, safe culturally, safe physically, safe in their environment, and safe with the process[viii].

It's a bit funny, but Sam Safety uses his five toes to remind him.

The five toes of the Safety-First Foot

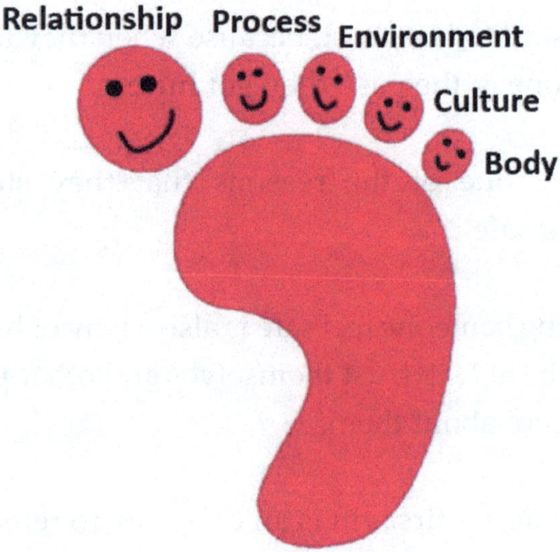

If we think about how to create each of the five types of safety, we can help someone feel calmer, less threatened and stressed.

When they feel calm and we talk, and they will be able to remember what we said.

1. Safe relationship

Creating a safe relationship with someone means being careful how you act and talk. Your actions and words should not make someone feel bad, less important, wrong, hopeless, worthless, or broken.

Sam Safety suggests that we make sure the person knows that no matter what has happened *to* them, they are special, and it is possible to heal and get better.

Sam Safety recommends that we treat the person who has experienced trauma with compassion, empathy and acceptance.

They also need to know that you won't hurt them physically, sexually, emotionally, spiritually, financially or mentally.

To prove this, you will need to be consistent, reliable, transparent, honest and available. If you say you will do something or you won't do something, you must keep your word.

2. Safe culturally

Creating cultural safety for someone means that you think about what culture and background you come from, and how that might be similar or different from the other person.

Sam Safety helps us remember that if you do things the way you prefer to do things, that may be different from someone else's cultural ways of doing things. That might make them feel uncomfortable and anxious because it is different and unfamiliar.

You can learn about what is important in another person's culture, and you can ask how they would like to do things.

It is important to demonstrate consideration of how other people might think and act, and to treat those things with respect.

Even if it seems strange to you, make sure you value what the they believe, and make time and space to do things in the way they feel comfortable.

3. Safe in the body

Often when people have been physically hurt,

they feel scared of the pain in their body. They may avoid thinking about certain parts of their body because it reminds them of being hurt.

Sam Safety recommends we do not touch a person, make sudden movements, or get too close to them, so we do not frighten them.

This may be different if they are family, but you should always ask first if it is okay.

A person's clothes and skin are physical boundaries between them and you.

You should treat that boundary with respect, so they can trust you not to do anything that will make them feel physically unsafe.

4. Safe environment

Sam Safety knows that it is important to people who have experienced trauma, that you are careful about what you can do to make the place or room you are in feel safe.

This includes thinking about whether a door is locked, noticing if people can hear what you are talking about or if they can watch you through a window.

Also make sure there is nothing dangerous nearby like a fire, sharp objects, a cliff edge, or busy road. Loud noises and unpleasant smells can also feel unsafe.

Think about how to make the space feel predictable, and comfortable. It may also help if you meet in the same place each time.

Talk about how they can make their home or work environment also feel safer.

5. Safe with the process

One of the things that can make it much easier

and safer for someone you are helping who has experienced trauma, is if you talk about the process.

When someone doesn't know what you are planning or what to expect, they can feel nervous and anxious.

It takes a few minutes to explain what you have planned. Then ask if it is okay and if they have any questions about the process. Or ask them what they would like to do.

Sam Safety says that it is wise to also let someone know that even when the process starts, they can choose to ask for a break, to do things differently, or to stop.

Let them know they can tell you if they don't want to answer some questions or do things you ask if they feel scared or upset by it.

An imaginary safe place

Another way to help a person feel safe on their own or with other people is to have an imaginary 'safe place' in mind.

You can help someone choose a safe place in their mind that they can use any time.

The place should not have other humans in it, but may have a special toy, pet or angel who is there to protect and look after them.

Make sure that when they imagine the safe place, it helps them to feel calmer.

To make it feel real, ask the person to notice what they can see, what they can hear, what they can smell, what they can touch and taste in their safe place.

You could also ask them to 'anchor' this feeling by squeezing their thumb and first finger together when they imagine their safe place.

Later, whenever they press their thumb and finger together it will act like a cue to remember their safe place.

For children you can also make or draw a picture or build a model in a shoe box of their safe place.

UNDERSTANDING TRAUMA WITH CHARLIE CHOOSEY

Charlie Choosey understands that someone who has experienced trauma needs to be offered choices

The gift that Charlie Choosey brings is that they know how horrible it is to be in a traumatic situation and have no control over what is happening.

To help someone recover, it is good to understand that they need to be allowed to have a sense of control over some decisions in their lives.

It is good for people who have experienced trauma to have the option to make their own choices when they are on their own, and with other people.

Some people grow up with people in a family who are very strict or mean or hurtful. They may have been told lots of things that aren't true about being an unlovable or ugly or stupid person.

Young people who have grown up in families like this might start to think that there is nothing they can do to change things[ix], and become very hopeless and depressed.

Charlie Choosey knows that when this happens to people when they are young, they learn to believe it, and stop having confidence in themselves.

That means they can also lose confidence in knowing how they feel or what they think or want. They often look to other people to tell them what to do.

Charley Choosey explains that when a person experiences something that is traumatic, they feel unsafe, and they don't have any control over what is happening.

In the middle of a frightening or painful experience, the person has no choice but to stay there and experience the pain.

Charlie Choosey says

Charlie Choosey says we can help someone learn how to trust themselves. They can learn to have confidence in knowing how they feel and think and what they want. We can help them by asking.

Charlie Choosey knows it is helpful to give children and young people choices when there is a decision to make[x].

You can ask what they prefer, and not give the answer or tell them what to do.

Charlie Choosey says

These steps can help someone build confidence to make their own decisions.

Step one: Start with two options

It may take a while for someone to feel confident in making their own decisions. They need time to learn to control what happens to them.

Making little decisions between two options is a way to start helping someone build confidence in their ability to make safe choices.

Example 1

"Would you like an apple or a banana?"

Example 2

"Would you prefer to meet on Thursday or Friday?"

A person lacking confidence in their own ability to make safe choices, may say they don't mind, and you can choose for them.

Charlie Choosey reminds us that giving a person choice is part of their healing.

Try not to decide for them.

Maybe ask again, and work together to help them learn how to make good choices for themselves.

Step two: Ask an open question

Once a person is feeling more confident that they can trust themselves to make simple choices safely, you can give them bigger choices. This means you can ask an 'open' question.

Example 1

"What time would you like to meet?"

Helping someone learn to make their own choices is a balance between too much choice and too little choice.

Charlie Choosey suggests you always keep in mind that you are working *together*, and the main thing to avoid is telling someone what to do.

You can offer some ideas, but try not to decide for someone.

Example 2

"Where would you like to sit?"

Remember that when the trauma was happening to them, the person was either told what to do against their will and they got hurt, or something bad happened to them that was outside their control.

Sometimes a person who has experienced trauma finds it difficult to make decisions together with someone else.

They might want you to tell them what to do, or they tell you what to do.

This happens because that is what they are used to. They haven't learned how to compromise or to find a solution that suits both people.

You can help someone to learn to grow out of these patterns of one extreme or the other, by encouraging them and showing them how to make joint decisions.

The drama triangle

One idea that is sometimes used to help understand the behaviour of someone who has experienced lots of trauma is called the 'drama triangle'.

There are three positions or roles a person can take on the drama triangle: The persecutor, the victim, and the rescuer.

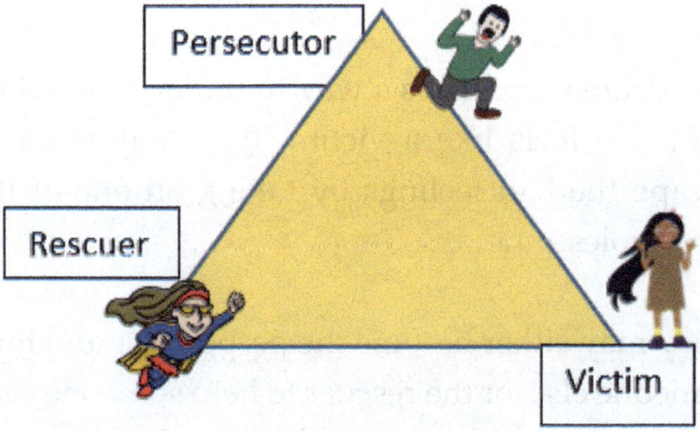

People can stay mainly in one role, or they can swap between roles depending who they are with or the situation.

Someone who has experienced trauma by being hurt by someone else might have thought of themselves as a victim.

The person who hurt them might be called the perpetrator. As the person supporting them, you could be in the role of rescuer.

Any person may have had a time in life when they felt like a victim. This feels horrible powerless, and frightening, and often people want to escape that feeling.

The drama triangle is a way to understand when someone feels like a victim, they may want to escape the bad feelings by taking on one of the other roles.

They may either become the perpetrator and hurt someone else, or the rescuer to help someone else.

Some ways a victim of trauma from being hurt by another person might respond using the drama triangle idea

Option A

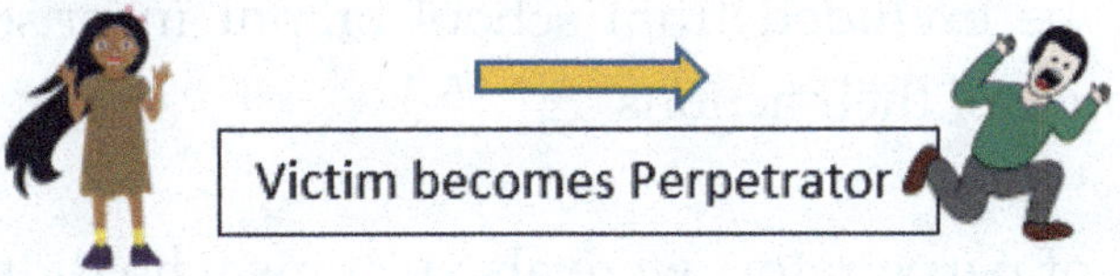

Option B

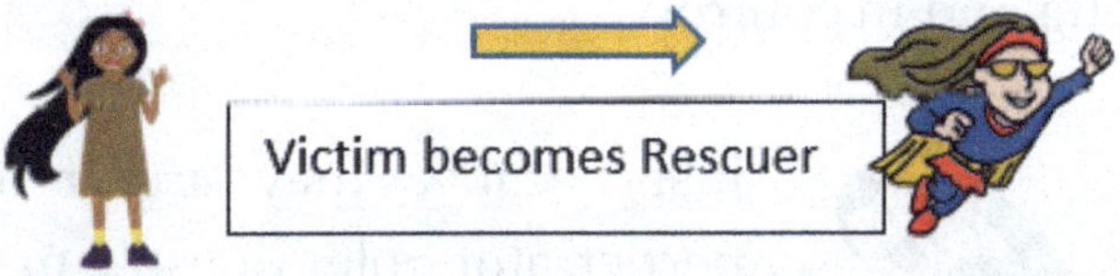

Option C

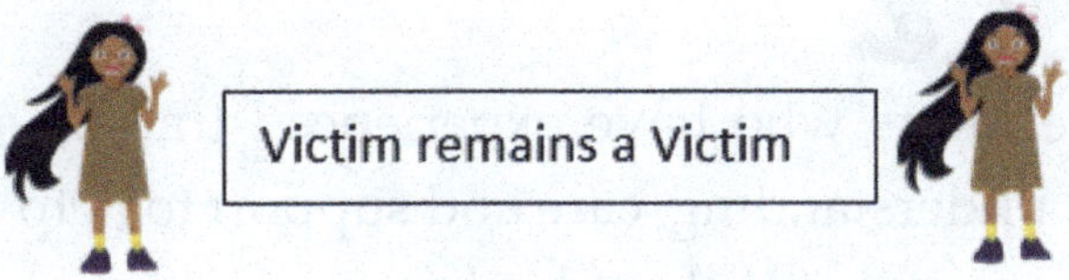

Perpetrators often still have a part of them inside that feels like a hurt victim

If a person chooses to escape being a victim by becoming a perpetrator, they may bully or hurt other people. Victims who become perpetrators may be excluded from school or put in prison because of their actions.

Lots of perpetrators were also victims who didn't have a chance to heal. By becoming a perpetrator, they escape feeling hurt and vulnerable and feel strong and in control.

Just because they are in the perpetrator role, doesn't mean the hurt victim part inside them has gone away or healed yet.

Perpetrators who have experienced trauma still need understanding, care and support to help the victim part inside them heal.

When that part heals, they don't have the same need to be a perpetrator to feel safe by being strong.

Sometimes victims choose jobs or take the role of rescuer in the family

Sometime trauma victims move into the rescuer role. Instead of feeling vulnerable and frightened as the victim, they can feel resilient, confident, and capable as a rescuer. They may move into situations or jobs where they can help other people.

Charlie Choosey reminds us they may still have part of them inside that was wounded by being a victim in the past. There may still be times now when they feel vulnerable and frightened and uncertain.

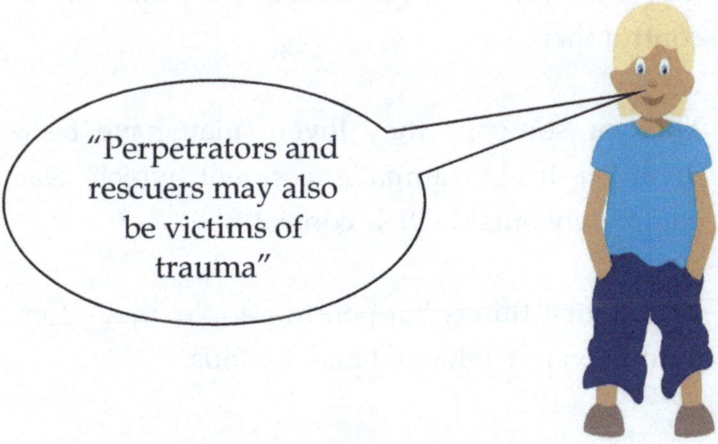

Just because they are in the rescuer role, doesn't mean that the hurt victim inside them has gone away or completely healed yet. Healing is a journey, and they can still be a good helper in the process.

Some victims of trauma do not move into either of these roles and remain thinking of themselves as a victim. They do not believe they can do anything other than continue to allow perpetrators to bully and hurt them, and rescuers to continue to try to help them.

Trauma can make people controlling

Charlie Choosey understands that when someone seems 'over-controlling' now, it may be because they were a victim of trauma in the past with no control then.

They or someone they loved, may have been involved in a traumatic accident which was completely outside their control.

When such things happen to people, they often become very frightened and anxious.

They think of people and the world as scary and unpredictable. They worry that something bad may suddenly happen to them again.

One way to cope with frightening feelings of uncertainty is to exert control over the things they can influence. This might mean they are very strict about what they eat or their gym schedule.

They may insist everything is kept a certain way and certain rules are followed.

Or someone who felt out of control when they experienced a trauma may control their home environment very carefully.

Having these rules for how to live, gives the person a feeling of security. They know that even if there are lots of things that happen in the world that are outside their control, there are some few things they can control within their immediate environment.

Charlie Choosey helps explains that when we know someone who is quite controlling, it might be because they have experienced a trauma in the past. Controlling things could be their way of coping with uncertainty.

We need to balance the Understanding Gang and The Change Family.

We need to understand why people who have experienced trauma act the way they do, before trying to change them.

We need to balance understanding first, and then change second.

PART THREE
THE CHANGE FAMILY

At the beginning you were introduced to everyone in the Understanding Gang and everyone in the Change Family. Remember that we said it was important to listen to everyone, because they all have some valuable gifts to share with us.

The Understanding Gang help you to make sense of the behaviour of someone who has experienced trauma. When you have understanding, you can show compassion, and can support them in a way that helps them rather than hurting them more.

Professor Brainy knows that we need to listen to everyone in the Understanding Gang before we talk to the Change Family.

We can't jump straight to listening to the Change Family without listening to the Understanding Gang first.

If we do, the person who has experienced trauma will probably feel that you don't accept them the way they are, and they must change for you to like them or care about them.

If we go straight to the Change Family, the person we are supporting will feel like we have not properly listened to them.
In other words, they will feel 'invalidated'.

They will feel like we don't like them the way they are because there is something that needs changing.

This is very hurtful for people who have experienced trauma, because they often already believe that they are not good enough or that they are unlovable.

The gift of wisdom that Professor Brainy offers you in relation to this topic is to first accept the person *as they are.*

In a counselling model called 'person centered' this is known as unconditional positive regard. In other words, it means that we think of the person in a positive way exactly as they are even if they never changed.

This is a special kind of care that is the most healing of all.

Remember this seesaw picture from the beginning of the book?

The word that Professor Brainy uses for keeping 'Understanding' and 'Change' in balance is *dialectic*. The word dialectic when supporting people who have experienced trauma means to keep a balance between 'acceptance' and 'change'[xi].

In other words, you both accept where a person is right now, as well as working towards a positive change that will be helpful for them in the future.

Another way to say this is to remember to use the word 'and' instead of 'but'.

Examples

- I am happy to see you ***and*** I am sad that you came late
- I understand that you didn't mean to do that, ***and*** I am willing to help you do it differently next time if you would like that
- I don't mind that you smoke, ***and*** I can help you quit if you want to

In this section, the Change Family take turns to share their special gifts with you, knowing that you have already spent some time with the Understanding Gang.

When we help someone who has experienced trauma, there might be some behaviours that they would like to change. Usually, they have started doing those things to help them manage the trauma symptoms.

Even if those things are harmful, whatever the person you are supporting has been doing to help them cope with their trauma symptoms so far, has to some extent, given them temporary relief from their distress.

It is best not to ask someone to stop these things straight away before they have any alternatives.

If we don't offer alternative ways of coping first before encouraging someone to stop their harmful ways of coping, the person is left with a gap of not having any tools or strategies to use to help themselves.

The Change Family invite you to offer support and understanding first before you teach them how to do something else instead.

To start with, the Change Family suggest you offer their gifts in ***addition*** to their current ways of coping rather than *instead of*.

Gradually the person can then become less reliant on coping strategies that are harmful or keeping them stuck, and little by little, learn to use the new skills instead.

CHANGING TRAUMA SYMPTOMS
WITH
BABY BRAVE

Baby Brave knows that for someone who has experienced trauma to change their symptoms they need to be brave

The gift that Baby Brave brings is that they she has no fear. Baby Brave never avoids people or things or feels scared of anything.

Baby Brave is amazing and shares the gift of facing things head-on. Baby Brave wants to learn and grow and always wants to ask questions and investigate things.

Baby Brave is so curious about what is going on, and crawls around all over the place examining and exploring things. Baby Brave gives the gift of courage and trust and confidence that even difficult things can get better.

One of the symptoms people experience after trauma is avoidance[xii]. This includes avoiding situations or 'triggers' that remind them of the trauma event.

It also means avoiding the thoughts and emotions that relate to the trauma situation.

Avoiding things keeps the problem going

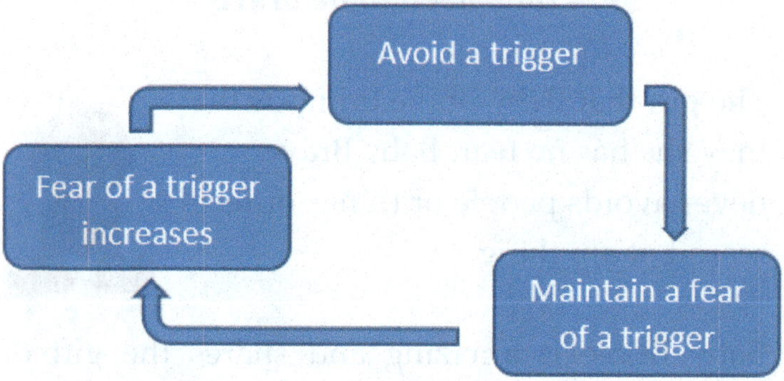

Avoidance is a psychological defense to try to get away from feelings of distress[xiii]. Apart from avoiding people, places, objects, music, and situations that are reminders of the trauma, people also use drugs and alcohol to try to avoid the thoughts and feelings inside them.

Baby Brave says

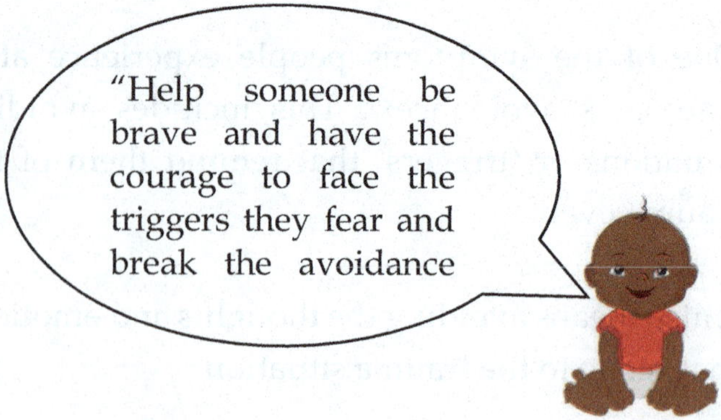

Avoiding things can make the suffering after experiencing a trauma last longer.

The problem with avoiding feared triggers, is that every time a person goes around this cycle, they risk increasing their original fear of the trigger[xiv]. This means the person can get stuck and trapped in an avoidance cycle.

The gift Baby Brave gives is to support the person you are helping to have the courage to be brave and face the trigger they are frightened of.

It is only when a person takes this courageous step to bravely face what they fear that they can break this cycle of avoidance and fear that keeps them trapped and stuck.

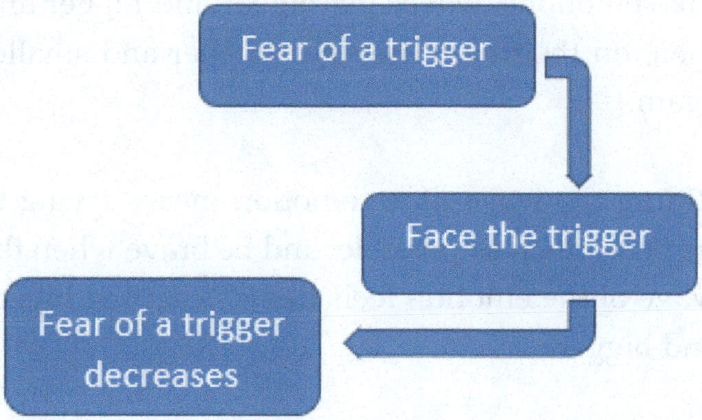

Surfing the feeling

Baby Brave is also keen to share with you the gift of surfing. This means that when a person has an urge to run away, or avoid a trigger they are afraid of, they don't.

Instead, they stay with the feeling and 'ride' it like a surfboard until the feeling reduces on its own.

This works because distressing feelings have a point at which they cannot go any higher. When they reach that point, they must start coming down again.

Like emotions, waves get bigger and bigger and then, on their own they get smaller and smaller again.

Riding the wave of an emotion means trying to relax as much as possible, and be brave when the wave of the emotion feels like it is getting bigger and bigger.

If you 'hold on' and ride the wave of the emotion and don't avoid it, you will find that on its own it starts to get smaller and smaller again.

When you think about the trauma or have a trigger, your emotions and heart rate go up and you feel worse, which makes it really tempting to try to avoid that trigger.

When you avoid it, those feelings start to go down and in the short-term you feel better. The problem is that you get into the habit of having to avoid every trigger to feel better.

Breathe through the feeling

Baby Brave gives another choice, which is that when the distressing feelings are almost at their highest and you want to get away and do something to avoid the feeling, just hang on a bit longer.

Breathe slowly and deeply until the feeling gets smaller again.

Instead of running away, if you breathe deeply and slowly, and be courageous like Baby Brave, then you can learn to cope with the feeling instead of avoiding it.

When you succeed in coping with the feeling when it is at its worst, you start a new cycle of positive feedback. You teach your body and emotions that after a certain point the feeling starts to get easier again.

You learn that you don't have to avoid the feeling to feel better, you can ride the feeling to feel better.

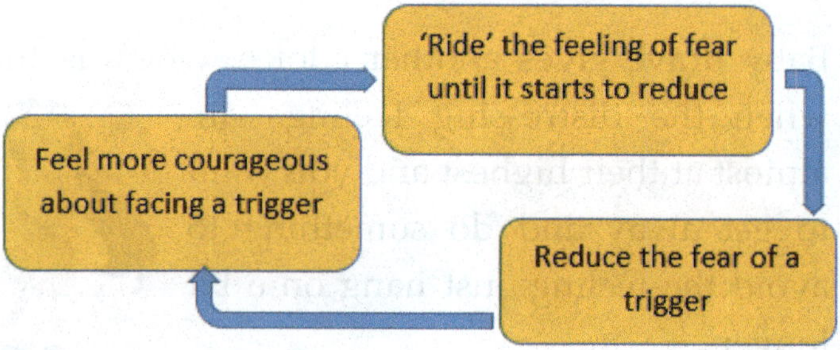

Each time you do this, you build confidence that you can cope with the next wave when it comes.

When you are nearly at the top and want to give up, remember that you will soon be on the downhill slope.

This is something a person can only really learn through experience, and it is the only way to break the avoidance cycle.

When you break the avoidance cycle, a new cycle of bravery is created, and you can escape the restriction of fear.

Take your time

Remember what Sam Safety from the Understanding Gang taught us at the beginning of this book, and don't push someone to face their fear too quickly.

This could be really overwhelming for someone and make them even more frightened. Be supportive and work on facing the fear little by little so that even though they must be brave, they know that you are helping them to do it.

Use mindfulness

Using mindfulness decreases avoidance[xv]. Some mindfulness skills that Baby Brave wants to share with you are 'being curious', 'floating' and 'turning towards'. These are like the skills you learn in mindfulness[xvi].

These skills help us to face up to triggers bravely instead of avoiding them

Baby Brave says

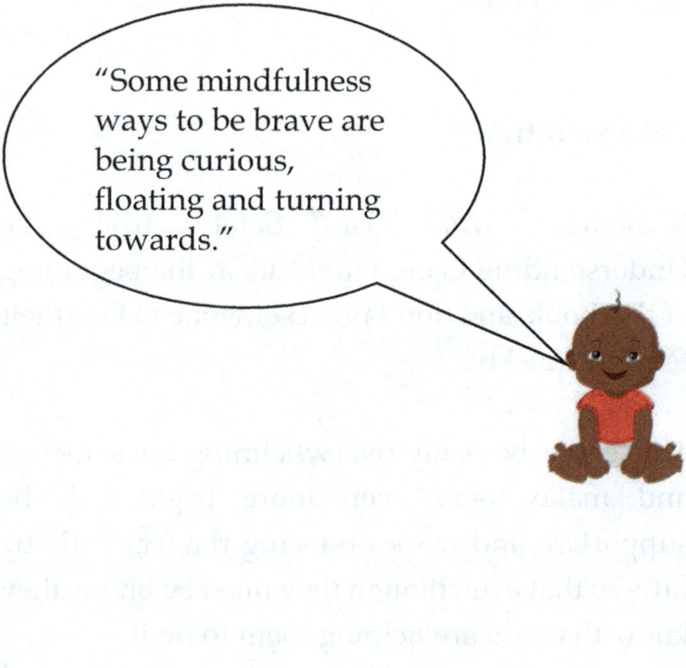

Being curious

Being curious means thinking of the thing that is painful or upsetting or scary as something to be investigated and explored. This can help you to be less frightened of it.

You could become curious about a place or a person[1] or a thought, a feeling, or a sensation in the body. Being curious means wondering more about it.

Some people like to imagine they are a detective gathering information.

Some people like to imagine themselves as an alien trying to learn about humans.

You could also think of yourself as a poet or an artist, looking at the feeling or the place with a creative perspective.

[1] NB – take care to make sure that there is no actual current risk from the person

Fighting with feelings or thoughts tends to make them stay longer.

Being curious helps you to be less frightened of the feeling that comes when you are reminded of the traumatic thing.

You could be curious about where in your body the feeling is, how big it is, or what colour or shape or size it is.

Sally Scared feels like the fear is a big orange spiky explosion in her chest.

When you start to be curious about the painful or scary feeling, it becomes more familiar, and it is easier to allow it to be there until it is ready to leave.

Floating

Floating requires an attitude of non-resistance. Instead of fighting against a feeling or thought we don't want, we 'float' along with it instead. Resistance involves tension and effort. Floating is the opposite of resistance.

Imagine the feeling of floating. Floating doesn't involve struggling, fighting, or avoiding.

You have to relax to allow yourself to float. Baby Brave likes to imagine herself floating in a bubble.

If you have ever tried not to sink in water, the best thing to do is to relax so that you can float on the surface.

Floating requires trusting and relaxing. Instead of becoming tense when you are reminded of the trauma, it is better to do the opposite.

When we relax, we are able to 'ride' the feeling or 'float' with the feeling until it reduces on its own.

There is a saying that
"What you resist persists".

When we are trying to get rid of a thought or feeling we don't like or want, we resist it. We struggle and fight against it.

We might force ourselves to try not to think about it, or try hard to think positive things instead.

This requires a lot of effort. Try floating instead of resisting.

Turning towards

When something is painful or frightening, our instinct is to avoid it or move away.

As Baby Brave explained to us, this only keeps the problem going, and usually makes it worse.

Turning towards the thing that is painful or scary is the opposite of avoidance. Being curious when you turn towards the pain can help make it less frightening.

Turning towards the place or thing that is difficult is the opposite of what you want to do, because when you do, it seems like the feelings of anxiety start to get worse.

You might turn towards a place you avoid, like a road where an accident happened (as long as it is safe to do so).

As Baby Brave explains, turning towards what we are scared of instead of away from it is the way to take control of the fear, and be able to grow past it.

Remember that the horrible feeling gets a little bit worse to start with when you turn towards the thing you are frightened of.

But then the feeling starts to get less again when it goes down the other side of the wave.

CHANGING TRAUMA SYMPTOMS WITH COUSIN CALM

Cousin Calm knows that for someone who has experienced trauma to change their symptoms they need to be calm

The gift Cousin Calm brings is that he is excellent at helping people feel calmer.

He gives lots of good advice about how to switch off from worrying about things and get a good night's sleep.

Cousin Calm is great to have around because being with him makes people feel better.

He gives the gift of companionship and makes sure no one feels lonely or left out.

Cousin Calm shows us that a little bit of stress is good for us, but too much is usually a problem and is harmful.

Look at this picture of the 'Stress Curve'[xvii].

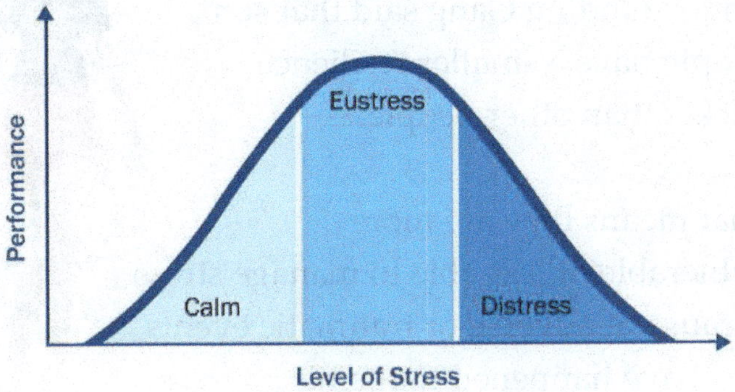

This picture shows along the bottom axis from left to right increasing levels of stress. On the vertical axis increasing performance from bottom to top.

The higher the curve, the more able someone is to do what they need to do. This picture shows that the more stressed someone is, the lower their ability to do what they need to do.

This means that keeping stress low is not only healthier, but it is also more effective.

Coping with stress

Penny Predictable from the Understanding Gang said that some people have a smaller resilience bucket than other people.

That means they are more vulnerable or less able to manage stress because of adverse or traumatic events that have happened to them.

Traumatic things or Adverse Childhood Events (ACEs) make someone's resilience bucket smaller than other people's buckets. They are more likely to struggle with difficult things.

So, when stressful things happen, their bucket gets filled up quicker, and they get overwhelmed quicker.

What we learned from Penny Predictable is that people who have experienced traumatic things in their life may feel exhausted and anxious with less stress than people who haven't had those terrible things happen to them.

She taught us that resilience is the opposite of vulnerability, and there are things we can do to help people increase their resilience.

Her gift was to explain that you can help people by ensuring that you are *predictable, consistent, and reliable.*

Cousin Calm explains how people who have experienced trauma can learn to be calmer in stressful situations.

The Window of Tolerance

Cousin Calm has a helpful diagram called the 'Window of Tolerance'[xviii].

This doesn't mean a window like one with glass where we can see outside.

The Window of Tolerance is more like a zone or area on a graph, like this one.

Window of Tolerance

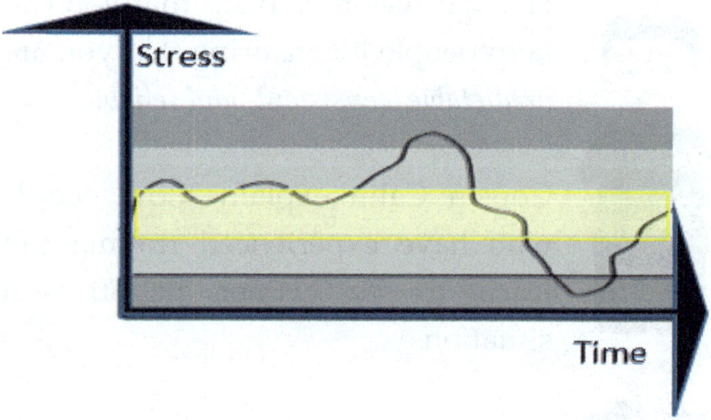

The best place to be is in the middle, with a 'middle' amount of stress.

Cousin Calm says

In this diagram, Cousin Calm shows us that when we are in the 'middle' range of stress, we are most productive and healthy.

Some people call this middle range 'eustress'[xix] because *eu* is Latin for 'good'.

In other words, a little bit of stress is good stress, but too much causes 'distress'.

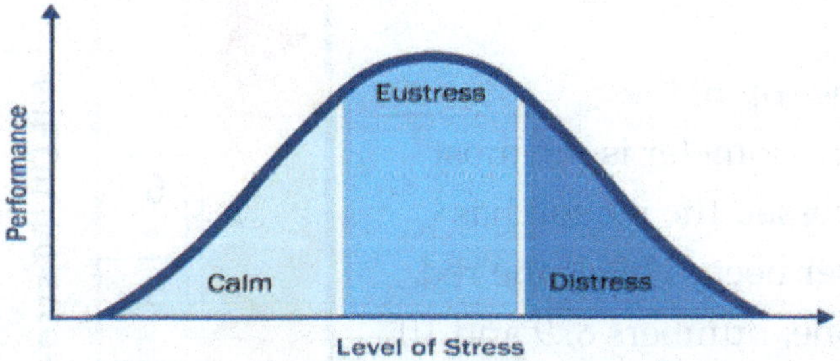

You can use the picture of a window or the stress curve to help people you are supporting understand that too much stress is problematic.

Now Cousin Calm will talk a bit more about what he has learned about how to calm yourself down when you are too stressed, and how to stay calm.

Calming down in stages when someone is VERY stressed

Cousin Calm knows that when someone is very stressed, the best way to calm down is to do it in stages.

Stressometer

Imagine you have a Stressometer.

The top of the Stressometer is the most stressed the person has ever been. This is the red zone; numbers 8, 9 and 10.

The bottom is not stressed at all. This is the green zone; numbers 1, 2 and 3.

To use the gifts from Cousin Calm, it helps to first check where on the Stressometer the person you are supporting is.

You can do this by asking this question.

"On a scale of 1 to 10, with 10 being the most stressed you have ever been, and 1 being not stressed at all, how stressed are you feeling right now?"

Or you could show someone a picture of your Stressometer and ask them to point to the level of stress they are feeling.

The following suggestions from Cousin Calm relate to whether the person is LOW, MEDIUM, or HIGH stress.

- High stress is the red zone.
- Medium stress is the yellow zone
- Low stress is the green zone

If the person starts in the HIGH zone, they can use some calming techniques from stage one.

When they are in the MEDIUM zone, they can use the stage two calming techniques.

The stage three LOW stress zone techniques are good at bedtime.

Stage one calming plan

Cousin Calm explains that when someone is in the HIGH stress zone, they need to start with a calming plan that will first use up some of the stress chemicals that are filling the body.

The best way to do this quickly is to do some exercise. The main stress chemical is adrenalin, which makes you feel like moving!

There are lots of things that someone can do to move their body around; Running, jumping, dancing, shaking, bouncing, rolling - anything that involves moving!

Sometimes adults feel embarrassed about jumping up and down if they are stressed at work, or somewhere where they don't think they can do something physical.

Having a little trampoline in the corner of the room might be a great thing to do for a few minutes each day or a game of football at lunch time.

Going out for a walk in a break or climbing up and down some stairs can be something physical to do that feels okay instead.

For people who are less physically mobile, swinging their arms can work, or fist bumps in the air.

Another way to get the stress chemicals down in the stage one calming plan is to give the body a shock with some cold air or cold water or ice.

This could be a cold shower, or splashing cold water on your face, wrists, or feet. An ice pack on the head, neck or hands could be used. Some people like to suck ice-cubes.

A fan blowing cold air, cold air conditioning, or going outside in cold weather are other ways to cool the body down.

Remember to avoid caffeine in energy drinks, coffee, tea and cola, and sugary foods and drinks. These act as stimulants and will mimic the feeling of stress.

Cousin Calm says

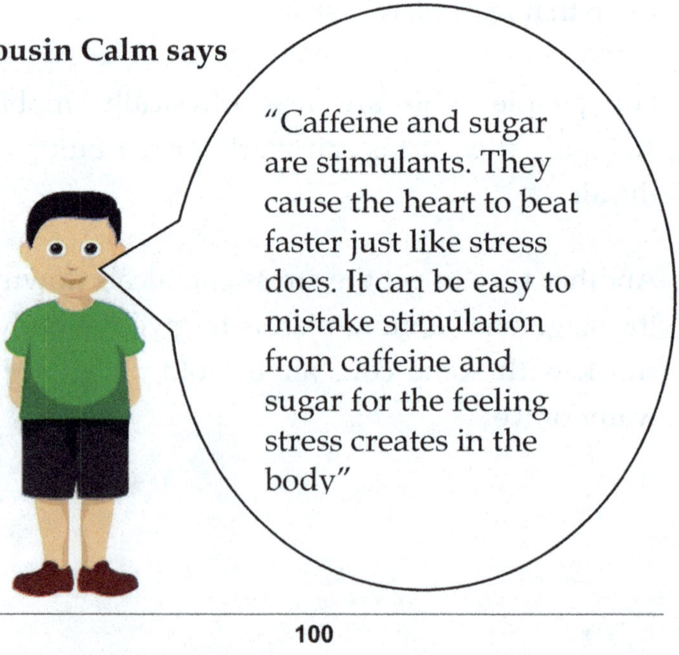

Stage two calming plan

Cousin Calm explains that when someone is in the MEDIUM stress zone, they need a calming plan that is a bit less physical.

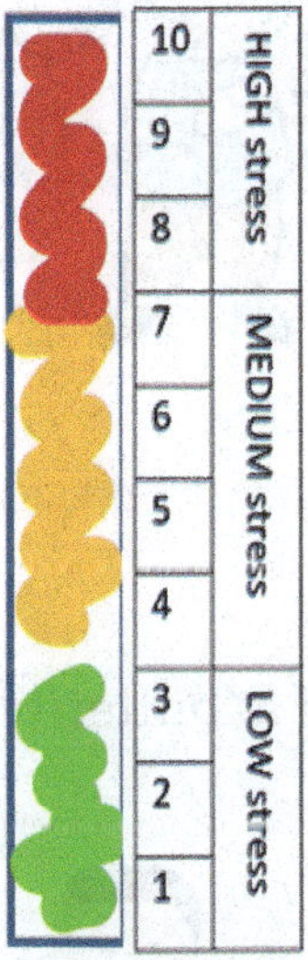

Remember that the techniques for this stage don't work very well if someone is in the high stress zone, so you should use those techniques first.

Check the person you are helping is in the MEDIUM zone by using the Stressometer. Also teach them how to check their Stressometer themselves.

Deep breathing

At this stage you can suggest deep breathing. Most people have heard of this, and it is easy to do. It is best to breathe in through the nose, down into the tummy or diaphragm. Watch for the tummy moving to check.

An important thing with deep breathing is to breathe ***out*** as fully as possible. A good way to make sure someone has breathed out fully is to blow the breath out.

Blowing out candles, blowing bubbles, blowing up balloons, or blowing a small ball across a table are all ways to make sure some good deep breathing is happening.

Butterfly hug

Cousin Calm also recommends doing a 'butterfly hug' at stage two.

You can also add breathing in and out deeply and slowly at the same time as doing the butterfly hug.

Show the person you are helping how to cross their arms over each other, with hands facing upwards on their chest or shoulders. Then tap each hand alternately.

This is especially good for people who have experienced trauma, because the tapping alternately with each hand helps the brain calm down as well as the body.

Earthing

At stage two, Cousin Calm recommends contacting the ground with bare feet or another part of the body. This is called 'earthing'. It is another way to help the body settle down.

Putting bare feet on the earth or grass or sand allows negative ions from the earth to pass through the skin. These ions reduce inflammation and help get rid of free radicals, which are unstable atoms in the body that cause aging and illness[xx].

Low key activities that don't need too much physical or mental energy such as knitting, painting, baking, or easy gardening can also be good relaxing things to do at stage two.

Positive affirmations

During stage two, you can also help someone to think of a short positive statement that they can tell themselves.

When repeated, this can help their mind from going around with lots of negative thoughts. Focusing on one simple thought, means that the brain is too busy to focus on anything else.

A helpful statement to say is "I'm okay" or "It's going to be alright". You can think of something similar. Encourage the person you are helping to repeat the phrase over and over out loud or in their mind.

Stage three calming plan

Cousin Calm explains that when someone is in the LOW stress zone, this is when they might want some help with really relaxing and getting to sleep.

Stress check

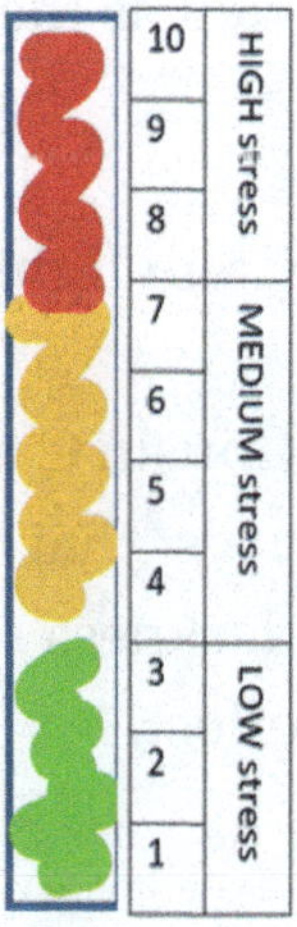

Use the Stressometer again to check whether someone is in the LOW stress zone. Then they are ready for stage three calming. Being warm can help.

A warm blanket, a warm drink or warm bath can help the body relax.

Calm music

Music is helpful at each stage of the calming plan if it is the right kind of music. Some music can make you feel like getting up and dancing, which would be useful to listen to if you are in stage one HIGH stress.

The useful kind of music for stage three calming is very gentle and quiet. You could ask the person you are helping to make their own playlist for each stage.

Music without words is better for stage three calming, so that the brain has a chance to rest as well as the body.

Calm lighting

Cousin Calm says that there are special cells in the eyes that are sensitive to light; and being in darkness or just closing your eyes has a calming effect.

The best thing to do if you are in stage three and trying to relax or sleep, is to be in a dark room and close your eyes. Some people like to cover their eyes with a mask to block out the light fully.

Keep it dark

Computers, TVs, and phones have bright screens that keep the brain active and awake, so it is helpful to not look at these bright screens when you are trying to calm down in stage three of the plan.

If you want to still use electronic devices, you can buy yellow glasses. Wearing these will block out most of the bright light from electrical devices that keep you awake.

Stretching, swinging, stroking

Some people like to do gentle stretching exercises to release tension in their muscles at stage three calming.

Simple repetitive motions such as swinging or rocking in a chair or stroking a pet are also excellent stage three calming activities.

Settle your body first then your mind

Think about settling your body down first, then give your mind something calm and simple to focus on. This could be a lightweight novel, listening to calm sounds like rain, watching an open fire or fish tank.

Neutral sounds like a background hum of air conditioning, or even a white noise machine can help attract the mind's attention without being too stimulating.

If you watch TV, choose something quiet, rather than watching a very emotionally stimulating programme such as a film with car chases and dramatic music.

The body and brain like routines, and if you train yourself with a routine to calm down, your body will automatically start to feel more relaxed when you start the routine.

Cousin Calm suggests that you choose three things that you always do in the same order. Do this every time you want to settle yourself down at stage three to relax or go to sleep.

Tips from Cousin Calm for stage three

- Have a warm bath with lavender oil, listening to calm music with low lighting.
- Change into comfortable PJs and sit in the rocking chair and read part of a novel.
- Turn the lights off and lie flat, stretch every muscle then relax.
- Breathe slowly, listening to the hum of the fan.

CHANGING TRAUMA SYMPTOMS WITH NANA NOTICING

Nana Noticing knows that for someone who has experienced trauma to change their symptoms they need to notice things

The gift that Nana Noticing brings is that she notices everything! Nothing gets past Nana Noticing.

She notices smells and sounds and tastes and the texture of things.

She notices how she is feeling and what she is thinking. She notices how she reacts to other people and situations.

Nana Noticing helps people to stay in the here-and-now and not to disconnect from float off into a daydream.

Dissociation

One thing people who have experienced trauma often do is something called dissociation. Everyone dissociates a little bit, and some people dissociate a lot.

Dissociation is on a continuum, with full awareness on one end and full dissociation on the other[xxi]. People can move up and down the scale at different times.

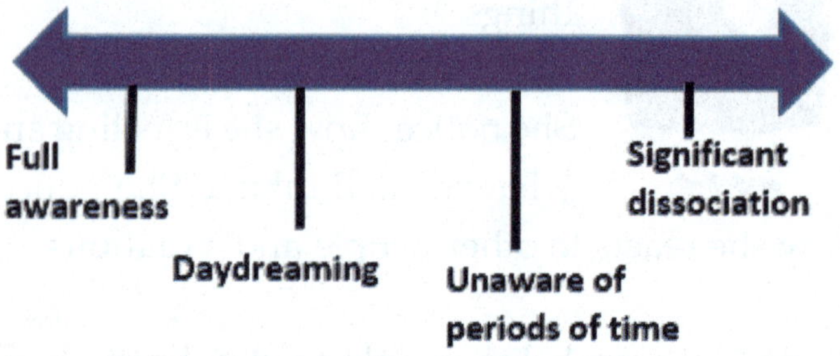

The word continuum means it is not that people either dissociate or they don't. It means dissociation is a smooth scale from no dissociation to dissociating often.

Nana Noticing has been talking to Professor Brainy and knows that the brain has part of it that works without us thinking about it called the unconscious. It also has part that works when we are aware of it called the conscious part.

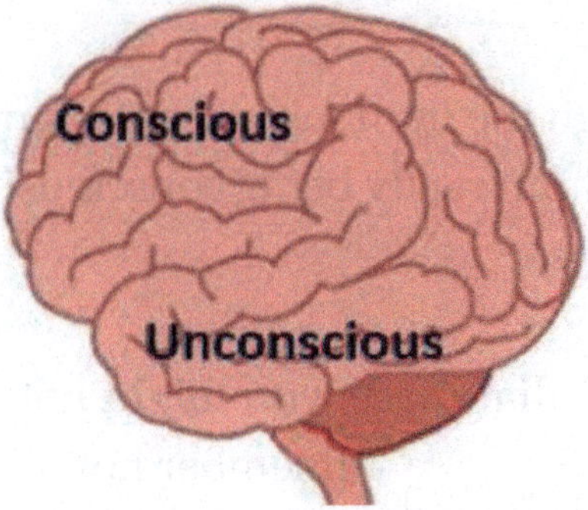

Things that are automatic such as breathing and heartbeat, are in the unconscious part.

Things we have choice and control over are in the conscious part, such as choosing to reach your arm out to pick up a cup.

Things that you do regularly can also become automated like driving along a particular route, or feeding the cat.

Automatic pilot

When a person is daydreaming or dissociating, they are mainly operating in the unconscious part of the brain. You could say that are on 'automatic pilot'.

You could 'go through the motions' of something you do regularly without really being consciously aware of doing it.

After driving to a familiar place, you might not

remember how you got there, because you have trained your body to drive with little conscious awareness.

Trauma and dissociation

When people experience trauma, sometimes they move into the unconscious mode of dissociation whilst the trauma is happening. This is called 'peri-traumatic' dissociation. *Peri* means during.

Dissociation during a trauma can be a very helpful adaptive process of the body and brain to keep you safe.

If the trauma involved something painful happening to the body, the brain might automatically cause that person to dissociate so that they are not as consciously aware of the pain.

So, in the moment of trauma, it can be a very helpful thing to happen.

However, dissociation can start to be a problem for some people when it happens often in their life, and it becomes a habitual way of avoiding physical, mental or emotional pain. For some people, they might even engage in harming themselves or others whilst in a dissociated state.

One of the gifts that Nana Noticing gives is to help people learn not to 'check out' and to switch into automatic pilot mode.

The 'defeat' response

Inside the body, there is a difference in the chemicals produced in dissociation than when a person in fight or flight mode.

In dissociation a chemical in the body causes the blood pressure to drop. Some experts call this is the *defeat* response[xxii].

Other chemicals in the body can make people get mixed up about space and time and what is real[xxiii].

This explains why when people have experienced something traumatic, they are unclear about how long the event was, what order things happened in, or the size of objects.

When someone dissociates during the trauma, they often also have gaps in their memory of what happened[xxiv].

Dissociation can happen to someone years after a traumatic event, whenever they see or hear or smell something that reminds them of what happened. These reminders are called 'triggers.'

For example, the smell of petrol might be a trigger for someone who was in a car accident. When a trigger happens, the person has an automatic fear response that is unconscious and outside their control.

Nana Noticing says

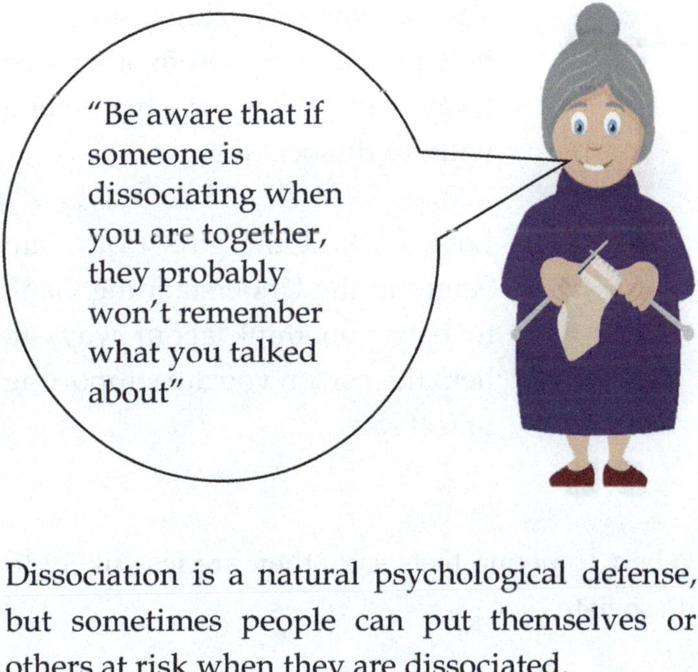

Dissociation is a natural psychological defense, but sometimes people can put themselves or others at risk when they are dissociated.

Also, if you are talking to someone who dissociates when you are together, they will not remember what you talked about. This means you will both have wasted your time. So, it can be helpful to learn ways to deliberately avoid dissociation.

Following Nana Noticing's advice can help stop the automatic unconscious dissociation mechanism. People often dissociate when they feel unsafe.

The gift Nana Noticing brings is to help people stay present, and to be aware of what is happening without dissociating.

Look back at the gifts from Sam Safety in the Understanding Gang to help you think about ways to help the person you are supporting to feel safe.

When someone feels safe, they are less likely to dissociate.

Safety and predictability

Look back at Penny Predictable to remind yourself how to be more predictable, reliable, and consistent with the person you are supporting to recover from trauma

It is usually safer for someone who has experienced trauma to engage in life without dissociating. They can remain aware and present to make good choices.

They can remember where they have been and what they have been doing. They can also listen and learn, without this automatic defense mechanism kicking in.

Using all your senses with Nana Noticing

Nana Noticing helps us learn to notice everything going on around us. This means using all five senses to smell, taste, touch, listen and see.

Nana Noticing teaches us how to be aware of our surroundings, as well as noticing what is going on inside.

Inside you are thoughts and emotions and physical sensations in your body.

These sensations can feel frightening for people who have experienced trauma, and they may not want to spend time noticing them.

However, noticing is a very helpful skill to heal and grow after trauma.

Nana Noticing and Baby Brave often share their gifts together, because noticing things can require being brave.

Nana Noticing explains that when you learn to notice what thoughts you are having, this can help you to feel less stressed or anxious or depressed[xxv].

First of all, we have to notice we have had a thought. We have to catch it!

Nana Noticing says

Just because a thought comes into your mind, it doesn't mean that it is a fact or that it is true.

When you catch thoughts and notice them, you can choose which thoughts to keep and which to let go of.

Noticing thoughts

One way to start to learn to notice your thoughts is to imagine they are like leaves floating past on a stream.

Nana Noticing suggests you don't judge your thoughts, just sit quietly like you would on the bank of a stream and watch the thoughts pass by.

Getting used to watching thoughts is a way to start discerning which thoughts are helpful and make you feel better and which thoughts are unhelpful and make you feel worse.

You can then choose which thoughts to allow your mind to spend more time on, depending on which thoughts will make you feel better.

When you use the gift of noticing that Nana Noticing offers, you can learn to choose what you want to give your attention to[xxvi].

You can be selective about noticing things that make you feel good and give less attention to things that make you feel bad.

PART THREE
PROFESSOR BRAINY

Professor Brainy introduced herself and the team at the beginning of the book.

All the people in the Understanding Gang and the Change Family have now shared their gifts with you to help you understand and support anyone you know who has experienced trauma.

You might be interested to know a little bit more about what happens in the brain when someone experiences a trauma.

This can help make sense why it is so difficult sometimes to move on with life afterwards.

PROFESSOR BRAINY LOOKS INSIDE THE BRAIN

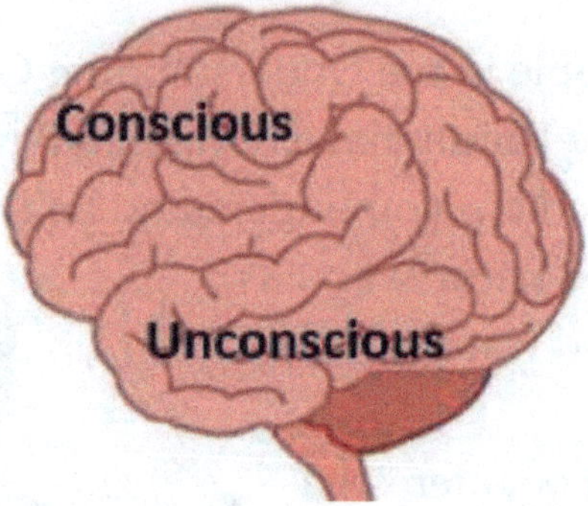

Remember that Nana Noticing invited Professor Brainy to talk about two parts of the brain when people dissociate. They are called the conscious and the unconscious.

When someone dissociates or 'zones' out' or daydreams, the unconscious part of the brain takes over. Now it is time to look inside the brain a bit closer to see what else goes on.

The way that Professor Brainy explains how the brain reacts to a traumatic or very stressful experience is to look inside three areas, the front (fore brain), the middle (mid brain) and the back (hind brain).

View of the brain from the side

The brain is in two halves, the left and right. These are also called hemispheres.

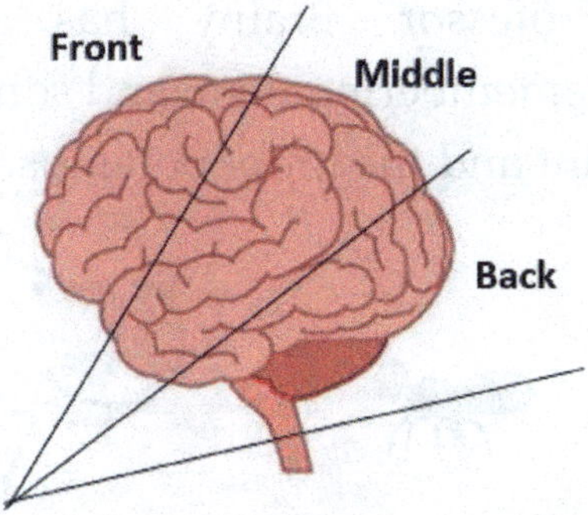

You might have heard people talk about how the right side of the brain is creative, and the left side is logical.

They both work together, and usually one part of the brain has a mirror image of itself on both sides.

This is the case for two important parts of the brain that are involved in creating and storing memories. They are called the amygdala and the hippocampus.

Amygdala and hippocampus

Professor Brainy has a funny way of remembering them and sometimes calls them the ant and the hippopotamus.

In the brain there is one amygdala on the left and one on the right of the brain. There is also one hippocampus on the left and one on the right.

This picture is taken from above the head looking down so that you can see the left and right at the same time. They are a mirror image of each other.

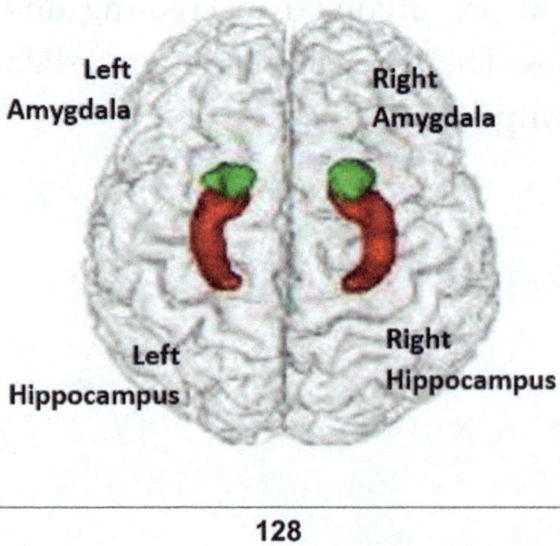

In the picture on the previous page, the amygdala are the two small parts in green, and the hippocampus are the two bigger parts in red.

Amygdala

The amygdala is quite small, which is why Professor Brainy gives it the nickname of an ant. Some people say it is shaped a bit like an almond.

The amygdala focuses on the emotional parts of a memory.

It is easier to remember things that if they are very emotional, and this is true of nice emotions as well as negative emotions[xxvii].

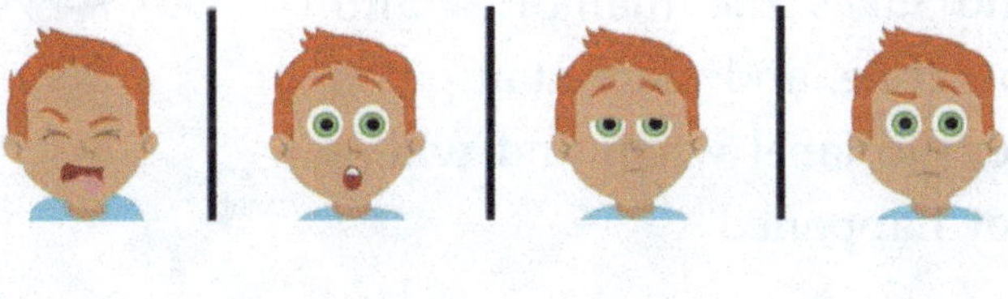

The amygdala takes in information from the five senses of taste, smell, touch, sight and hearing, and 'codes' that information as an emotion memory.

Hippocampus

Each side of the hippocampus is slightly bigger than the amygdala and is positioned very close to it.

Professor Brainy gives them the nickname of a hippopotamus. Some people think they look a bit like a sea horse.

The main job of the hippocampus is to store the memories so that they can be accessed later.

Imagine it a bit like a librarian who takes the memories and puts time, and place stamps on them to label when and where they happened.

The librarian in the hippocampus gets the memories nicely organised and filed away, so that we know where to find them when we want to remember something.

The amygdala and hippocampus must work closely together. The amygdala can gather information from the different senses in the body, and the hippocampus organises them into the memory library.

It is also one of the places in the brain where new brain cells are made through a process called 'neurogenesis' which means that the hippocampus is also very involved in learning new things.

Fear

Professor Brainy explains that because the amygdala is sensitive to emotion, if something scary happens, it can cause problems with memory.

When we are scared, we forget things.

To prove this, some scientists did an experiment where they put some rats near to a cat.

You might think this was a bit mean[2], because the rats were very scared that the cat would eat them.

What the scientists found out was that when the rats were frightened, they forgot what they had just learned[xxviii].

Trauma memory

The amygdala is good at remembering the emotion part of a memory but not noticing other details about the event.

Amygdala		
Good with emotion		Bad with details

This makes sense because one of the main jobs of the amygdala is to look out for danger and act as the brain's alarm system.

---

[2] Scientists aren't allowed to do scary things to humans any more, but they are allowed to do experiments like this on animals

It tends to take in the overall picture and main emotional context to check whether the thing that is happening is dangerous or safe.

The hippocampus is good at noticing and remembering details, and the timeframe. However, it is not good at recalling of the emotions connected with that situation.

Hippocampus		
Good with detail		Bad with emotions

It is good that each part has a specific job that it does well. This is usually fine when the amygdala and hippocampus are relaxed and communicating well with one another.

They make a good team and complement one another's strengths and weaknesses.

How memories go wrong in a trauma

The problem is that when a traumatic thing happens, a breakdown in communication can happen. The amygdala is overwhelmed with information from the five senses.

In situations of danger there are often too many physical sensations, lots of different sights and sounds and smells and sometimes tastes as well.

The poor amygdala can get completely suffocated with all these sensory pieces of information and doesn't have time to pass on all the information to the hippocampus to organise in the memory library.

Trauma memory metaphors

- It is a bit like an electrical circuit that gets overloaded and blows a fuse.

- Or like an assembly line in a factory that speeds up too much and the machinery doesn't have time to put all the products in the boxes.

- Or you could think of a conveyor belt at the airport with all the suitcases on, that goes too fast, and they all fall off in a mixed-up pile.

- Or when lots of things are shoved in a cupboard without care, and they fall out when you open the door.

Professor Brainy explains how trauma memories get mixed up

Professor Brainy explains that when a person recalls traumatic memories, they might end up with a big jumble of emotions and fragments of memories, with bits missing or in the wrong order.

Trauma memories are not properly organised into a sequence or labelled with the time and date like other kinds of memories.

They are a lot messier than the librarian in the hippocampus would like.

Also, the hippocampus is directly affected by stress hormones that are released during a traumatic experience and this causes the hippocampus to be less accurate in recording and labelling the timeframe of events[xxix].

When someone who experienced a trauma tries to remember what happened, events can be mixed up in the order they happened, or there can be parts missing from the memory.

The brain will naturally try to sort out the jumble through dreams by trying to piece together the fragments and make sense of them. It can be quite tiring physically, mentally and emotionally.

It can also take quite a long time to sort out after the traumatic event is over.

Even though the brain tries to sort out the pieces of memory on its own, sometimes it needs help. A counsellor or someone to talk with to help organise the pieces might be necessary.

A helpful part of counselling is to help the hippocampus put a proper 'end' date on the trauma memory, to clearly separate it from the present time.

Knowing how the memory gets disrupted like this is helpful for people involved in interviewing eyewitnesses for police investigations, refugee applications, and insurance claims for example.

The Autonomic Nervous System (ANS)

The autonomic nervous system is made up of two parts. First is the sympathetic part which is designed to get us moving. This is also called flight and flight.

The second is the parasympathetic part which is to calm us down. This is also called rest and digest.

Sympathetic. Fight or flight

The sympathetic system is activated when someone needs to get up and go. Professor Brainy has a nickname that it is the **S**tand-up part, because you have to stand up to get ready to fight or run away.

The body is designed to be able to release chemicals including adrenalin and cortisol into the bloodstream when there is a need to quickly jump out of the way of danger, or to protect yourself from harm.
This is sometimes called the fight / flight reflex.

However, if the body continues to stay in a state of high alert for long periods of time, the cells in the body can get damaged and worn out.

Parasympathetic. Rest and digest

The parasympathetic system is activated when someone needs to calm down and relax. Professor Brainy has a nickname that it is the **P**arachute part because a parachute helps you float down safely.

As soon as the danger has passed and it is safe again, the body engages the calm down system which is also sometimes called the rest / digest reflex.

All of this usually happens automatically.

The problem is we sometimes worry too much about things in life, or keep thinking about something painful or upsetting that happened in the past.

When we worry about the future or the past, we stop the body from its natural process of homeostasis and getting back into balance. This can make us ill.

Staying in balance

The word used when the body regulates itself to stay in balance is homeostasis.

When people have experienced trauma, they can't help being automatically triggered into a sympathetic, fight or flight response. The parasympathetic system is much less active, because it constantly receives messages that there is danger and it is not needed.

Whilst they are healing, people who have experienced trauma benefit from learning ways to train the parasympathetic, calm down system to switch back on.

This is like manually overriding an automatic system that isn't working properly.

The three layers of the brain

So far Professor Brainy has explained about how part of the way the brain works is conscious and part of it is unconscious. She also explained that the brain is in two halves, the left and right hemispheres.

Professor Brainy also said that there are three parts of the brain. These are called the front, middle and back.

Although the brain is divided into front, middle and back, these parts are also called, fore, mid and hind. Sometimes they are called neocortex, limbic and reptilian.

A more accurate way to think about these three parts is that they are like brain layers. The picture below is of a brain from a side-on angle, so we can see how these three parts are in layers.

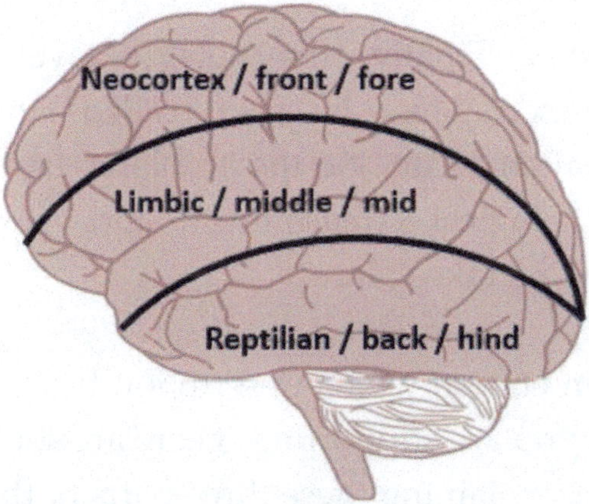

Sometimes this is called the triune brain because *tri* means three in Latin. The brain is in three parts that make up one whole.

Reptilian. You can see that deep at the bottom part the brain is the 'reptilian' system. It is the oldest part, and is connected to the brain stem at the top of the spinal column. It is the instinctive part of the brain.

Limbic. The middle layer is called the 'limbic' system'. It is also called the mammalian part. The amygdala and hippocampus are in here. It is the emotion part of the brain.

Neocortex. Finally, the outside layer is the 'neocortex'. This is also called the neo-mammalian brain, or the thinking brain. It is where logical reasoning and executive functioning takes place.

You can choose which description best suits the person you are supporting. There are some other ways of explaining these three parts of the brain, depending on the person' age, culture and the resources you have available.

One idea is to use your hand to model the three parts of the brain.

Hand model of the brain

This is a way of describing the three parts of the brain and what they do in a simple way using your hand[xxx].

Step One Hold your hand open wide and explain the three parts of the brain numbered in the diagram.	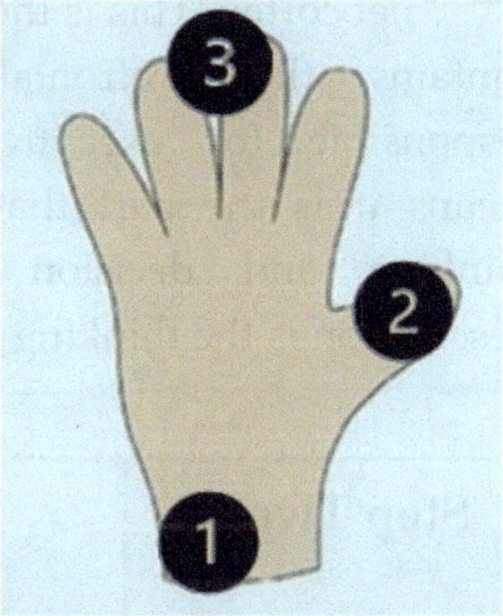

1 **The hind brain and brain stem.** This is also called the reptilian part. It is deep inside and connects the brain to the spinal column and regulates mainly autonomic responses such as breathing and heart rate. Mostly these processes happen unconsciously. A simple description is the instinctive brain.

2 **The mid brain.** This is also called the limbic system. This is the emotion regulation part of the brain that contains the amygdala and hippocampus. A simple description is the emotion brain.

3 **The fore brain.** This is also called the neocortex. This is the part of the brain that contains the prefrontal cortex which is responsible for executive functioning. That means it is the part that engages in rational thinking and decision making. A simple description is the thinking brain.

Step Two Tuck your thumb in front of your hand. Then fold your fingers over the top of your thumb.	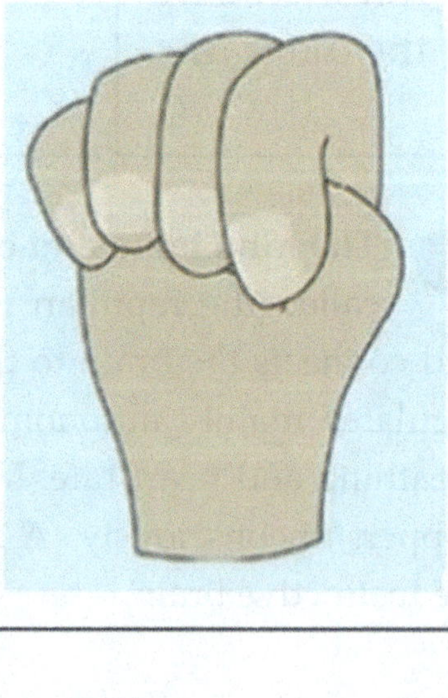

Describe how the emotional part of the brain is tucked inside the thinking part. The thumb part (limbic system) acts like an alarm. It is sensitive to information from the five senses (taste, touch, sight, hearing, smell). When the amygdala notices something picked up by one or more of these senses that seems dangerous it sets off an alarm.

Emotionally, this feels like terror, fear, or anxiety. The emotion of fear is triggered by the amygdala inside the limbic system part of the midbrain.

Step Three Flip the fingers up in the air to show how the thinking part of the brain 'flips its lid' when stressed.	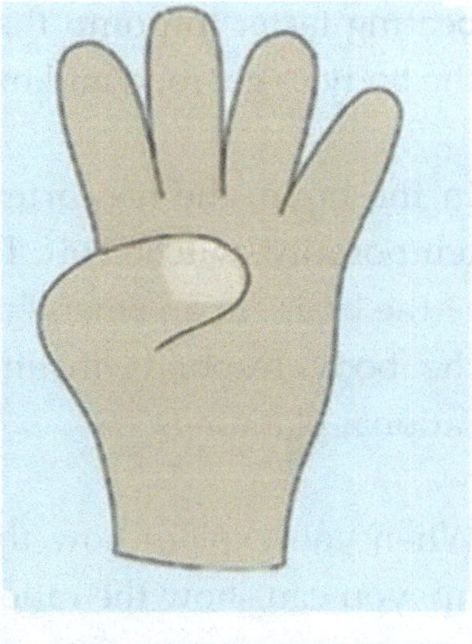

When the alarm goes off inside the brain, it thinks there is danger. The body and brain quickly move into fight/flight mode. The sympathetic nervous system takes over. This is the part of the autonomic nervous system that gets the body ready to escape, or to defend itself.

Inside the rest of the body lots of things are happening. The blood flow to digestion is temporarily reduced so that digestion stops, and the lungs get ready to take in more oxygen.

The breathing rate increases, and the heart starts beating faster to pump the blood quickly round the body to get food and oxygen to all the cells.

In the brain, the neocortex, or the fore brain is temporarily switched off. This is the thinking part of the brain. In an emergency it is not needed, as the body responds instinctively instead of by rational planning.

When you explain how the thinking brain flips up, you can show the rational thinking bit of the brain is no longer active. This is why people forget what to say or can't make rational decisions when they are scared or stressed.

Explaining the brain's response to trauma helps people realise they are not broken, and they are not to blame

In this section Professor Brainy showed how the brain works when it is stressed or experiences something very frightening or traumatic.

She knows that it can be very helpful to explain this to the person you are supporting who has experienced trauma.

Lots of people blame themselves for not doing something different when they were in the middle of the trauma.

Explaining how the brain works, and especially that the thinking part switches off when the person is in danger, can help a person to realise that it wasn't their fault that they responded as they did.

Knowing this information can often help people to be kinder to themselves when they realise that everyone's brain works like this, and it is a normal defense mechanism.

PROFESSOR BRAINY EXPLAINS GOING TO THE DOCTOR

When you go to the doctor to talk about any physical or mental health difficulties, the doctor will use a big book like an encyclopedia to look up the symptoms you are experiencing to make a diagnosis.

There are two books that doctors use depending on which country you live in. The first book is the Diagnostic and Statistics Manual (DSM) which is written by the American Psychiatric Association. The second book is the International Classification of Diseases (ICD) written by the World Health Organisation.

Professor Brainy thinks it is a good idea that you know a little bit about both. They have a lot of similarities and a few differences and get updated every few years. The latest version of the DSM is version 5, and the latest version of the ICD is version 11.

Trauma and stressor-related disorders

Lots of people recover from traumatic experiences and don't need to ask the doctor for extra help. However, if someone continues to have problems, the doctor will decide which diagnosis is most appropriate. In the DSM there is a chapter called 'Trauma and Stressor-Related Disorders'.

There are seven categories of diagnoses that are specifically about symptoms caused by experiencing a traumatic or stressful event. One of these is Post Traumatic Stress Disorder (PTSD). For a doctor to make a diagnosis of PTSD, they will check that the person has first had an experience that is classified as traumatic according to the DSM criteria. This is called Criterion A.

Criterion A. The traumatic event

The doctor first checks to see if the symptoms you are experiencing are because of a traumatic event or series of events. A traumatic event is described in a particular way in the table below.

Symptom cluster		Description
A	Exposed to actual or threatened violent death, serious injury or accident, or sexual violence	The person had one of these things happen to them or they saw it happen to someone else. Or they heard that one of these things happened to a family member or close friend. Or someone who repeatedly encounters trauma in their work.

Criterion B. Re-experiencing the trauma

The next questions they ask will be to find out whether you are experiencing any of the four main clusters of symptoms that people with PTSD have[xxxi].

The doctor will want to know if these symptoms started at the time or shortly after the traumatic event.

Symptom cluster		**Description**
B	Recurrent experiences of the event	The person keeps remembering the traumatic event in dreams at night and in the day. Often it feels like it is happening again which is called a flashback.

Criterion C. Avoiding trauma reminders

Any reminders of the trauma can cause the memories to flood back and feel like it is happening all over again. Because of this, people often try hard to avoid any reminders or triggers.

Symptom cluster		Description
C	Avoidance	Often people find their memories and stress levels get worse if they think about the traumatic event or if they see or hear or smell anything that reminds them of what happened. Because of this people avoid any thoughts, places, and memories about the event much as possible.

Criterion D. Negative thought and affect

Feeling anxious, stressed or having depressed thoughts is common in many other mental health diagnoses. However, it is also included as one of the criteria for a PTSD diagnosis.

Symptom cluster		Description
D	Negative thoughts and emotions	Emotionally, people can feel anxious, worried, fearful, and depressed and sad after experiencing a traumatic event. Their thinking can also become negative, maybe blaming themselves or others.

Criterion E. Increased stress and anxiety

One of the symptoms that is most noticeable in someone who has experienced a trauma, and still hasn't got over it, is hypervigilance. This is a word that means someone is constantly on high alert looking for signs of danger everywhere.

Symptom cluster		Description
E	Increased arousal	Arousal means an increase in feeling stressed, anxious, A person might be irritable or angry, and may do impulsive risky things. They may also be finding it difficult to relax or sleep well.

Criteria F, G and H.

The last few things the doctor will check include whether these symptoms have lasted more than a month, as many people feel better within this time. The doctor will also check if the symptoms are causing distress and making it difficult to do usual things in life, and that the symptoms have not been caused by something else.

Symptom cluster		Description
F	Symptoms more than a month	Lots of people have symptoms for a few weeks and gradually start to feel better. If you are still struggling after four weeks, the doctor may suggest you get some extra help.
G	Distress and impact on daily life	The doctor will also check if the symptoms from B-E are causing you to be upset and not be able to do your usual daily activities such as work or study or looking after your family.
H	Not caused by something else	Finally, the doctor will just check that there is no other medical reason for the symptoms.

Professor Brainy has read lots of research about how doctors diagnose PTSD. The research says that doctors don't always recognise when someone has PTSD.

Even if you are not a doctor, you might notice that someone you are supporting is experiencing these symptoms[xxxii].

The ICD-11

Remember Professor Brainy said that there were two books that doctors use. The other one that we have not talked about yet is the ICD-11[xxxiii].

Version 11 of the ICD has a new kind of PTSD category in it that has not existed officially before.

It is called Complex Post Traumatic Stress Disorder (C-PTSD).

Complex PTSD (C-PTSD)

Complex PTSD is likely to be diagnosed when someone has experienced repeated trauma such as childhood sexual or physical abuse, child soldiering, slavery, torture, war, or interpersonal violence.

When a doctor is making a diagnosis, they may also be looking for a group of another three symptoms, which are called 'disturbances in self-organization' (DSO).

This diagram[xxxiv] shows the same symptoms of PTSD in the ICD-11 for PTSD are used, with the addition of three extra ones for C-PTSD.

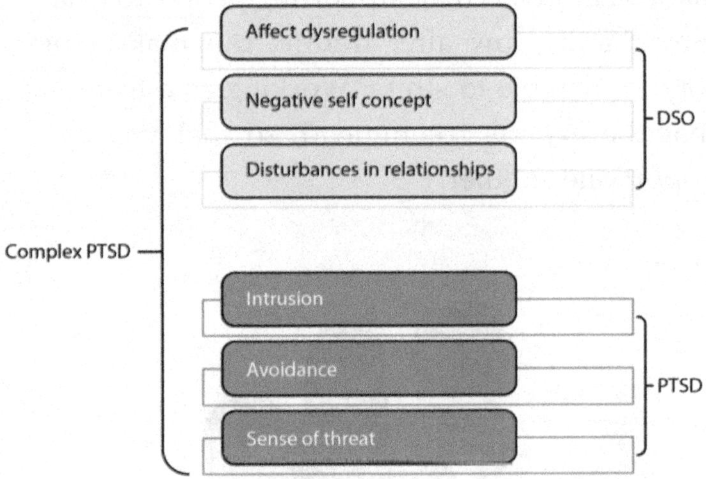

The three extra components of disturbances in self-organization are:

- persistent difficulty managing emotions[3]
- thinking negatively about yourself, including shame, guilt, and failure[4].
- having significant problems in relationships[5] with other people.

---

[3] Affect dysregulation
[4] Negative self-concept
[5] Disturbances in relationships

Working together as a team

One of the reasons that Professor Brainy works together with the Understanding Gang and the Change Family, is that supporting people to heal, recover and grow after trauma can make you more vulnerable to stress. Working as a team is what the experts recommend, so that you can support one another.

References

[i] Greer, A. (2021). Trauma responsive care model: An Aotearoa New Zealand research informed practice model for residential group homes. *Aotearoa New Zealand Social Work, 33*(1), 81-93.

[ii] Zubin, J., & Spring, B. (1977). Vulnerability: a new view of schizophrenia. *Journal of Abnormal Psychology, 86*(2), 103.

[iii] Bonnano, G. (2009). *The other side of sadness: What the new science of bereavement tells us about life after a loss.* Basic Books.

[iv] *Oxford English Dictionary* (2021). Retrieved from https://en.oxforddictionaries.com/definition/resilience

[v] Richardson, G. E. (2002). The metatheory of resilience and resiliency. *Journal of Clinical Psychology, 58*(3), 307–321.

[vi] Bath, H. (2008). The three pillars of trauma-informed care. *Reclaiming Children and Youth, 17*(3), 17–21.

[vii] Janoff-Bulman, R. (1992). *Shattered assumptions: Toward a new psychology of trauma.* The Free Press.

[viii] Based on a framework in Kiyimba, N. (2020) Trauma-informed Mindfulness: A guide to one-to-one work. Chester University Press

[ix] Rutter, M. (2012). Resilience as a dynamic concept. *Development and psychopathology, 24*(2), 335–344.

[x] Perry, B. (2006). Applying principles of neurodevelopment to clinical work with maltreated and traumatized children. In N. Webb (Ed.), *Working with traumatized youth in child welfare* (pp. 27–52). The Guilford Press.

[xi] Linehan, M. M. (2018). *Cognitive-behavioral treatment of borderline personality disorder*. Guilford Press.

[xii] American Psychiatric Association (APA) (2013). *Diagnostic and statistical manual of mental disorders* (5th ed.). APA.

[xiii] Palm, K. M., & Follette, V. M. (2000). Counseling strategies with adult survivors of sexual abuse as children. *Directions in Clinical and Counseling Psychology, 11*, 49–60.

[xiv] Clark, D. M., Ball, S., & Pape, D. (1991). An experimental investigation of thought suppression. *Behavior Research and Therapy, 29*, 253–257.

[xv] Brown, K.W., Ryan, R.M., & Creswell, J.D. (2007) Mindfulness: Theoretical foundations and evidence for its salutary effects. *Psychological Inquiry, 18*(4), 211–237.

[xvi] Follette, V., Palm, K. M., & Pearson, A. N. (2006). Mindfulness and trauma: Implications for treatment. *Journal of Rational-emotive and Cognitive-behaviorTherapy, 24*(1), 45–61.

[xvii] Yerkes R. M., Dodson J. D. (1908). The relation of strength of stimulus to rapidity of habit-formation. *Journal of Comparative Neurology and Psychology*. 18(5), 459–482.

[xviii] Siegel, D. J. (1999). *The developing mind*. Guilford Press.

[xix] Lazarus, R. S. (1974). Psychological stress and coping in adaptation and illness. *The International Journal of Psychiatry in Medicine, 5*(4), 321–333.

[xx] Ober, C., Sinatra, S. T., & Zucker, M. (2010). *Earthing: the most important health discovery ever?* Basic Health Publications, Inc.

[xxi] Braun, B. G. (1988). The BASK model of dissociation. *Dissociation, 1*(1), 4–23.

[xxii] Perry, B. D., Pollard, R. A., Blakley, T. L., Baker, W. L., & Vigilante, D. (1995). Childhood trauma, the neurobiology of adaptation, and "use-dependent" development of the brain: How "states" become "traits". *Infant Mental Health Journal, 16*(4), 271–291.

[xxiii] Resick, P. A. (2014). *Stress and trauma (Clinical psychology: A modular course)*. Psychology Press.

[xxiv] van der Kolk, B. A. (1996). The complexity of adaptation to trauma: Self-regulation, stimulus discrimination, and characterological development. In B. A. van der Kolk, A. C. McFarlane, & L. Weisaeth (Eds.), *Traumatic stress: The effects of overwhelming experience on mind, body, and society* (pp. 182–213). Guilford Press.

[xxv] Marchand, W.R. (2012). Mindfulness-based stress reduction, mindfulness-based cognitive therapy, and Zen meditation for depression, anxiety, pain, and psychological distress. *Journal of Psychiatric Practice. 18*, 233–252.

[xxvi] Tang Y. Y., & Posner M.I. (2009). Attention training and attention state training. *Trends in Cognitive Science, 13*, 222–227.

[xxvii] Hamann, S. (2001). Cognitive and neural mechanisms of emotional memory. *Trends in cognitive sciences, 5*(9), 394-400.

[xxviii] Diamond D. M., Fleshner M., Ingersoll N., and Rose G. M. (1996) Psychological stress impairs spatial working memory: relevance to electrophysiological studies of hippocampal function. *Behavioural Neuroscience*. 110, 661–672.

[xxix] Rothschild, B. (2010). *Eight keys to safe trauma recovery. Take-charge strategies to empower your healing*. W. W. Norton & Company Inc.

[xxx] Siegel, D. J. & Bryon, T.P. (2011). *The Whole Brain Child*. Constable & Robinson Ltd.

[xxxi] American Psychiatric Association (APA). (2013). *Diagnostic and statistical manual of mental disorders (5th ed.)* (DSM-5). Author. American Psychiatric Association (APA).

[xxxii] Brewin, C.R., Fuchkan, N., Huntley, Z., Robertson, M., Thompson, M., Scragg, P., d'Ardenne, P. & Ehlers, A. (2010). Outreach and screening following the 2005 London bombings: usage and outcomes. *Psychological Medicine, 40*(12), pp. 2049–2057.

[xxxiii] World Health Organisation (WHO) (2018). International Classification of Diseases, 11th

Revision (ICD–11) Retrieved from https://www.who.int/classifications/icd/en/

[xxxiv] From Kiyimba, N. (2020). *Trauma-informed Mindfulness: A practitioner guide for one-to-one work*. Chester University Press

Made in the USA
Las Vegas, NV
27 May 2024

90388631R10095